My Sister's
Cancer

How Prayer and Faith Sustained Us

Nancy Goulet

WestBow
PRESS
A DIVISION OF THOMAS NELSON

WestBow Press books may be ordered through booksellers or by contacting:

WestBow Press
A Division of Thomas Nelson
1663 Liberty Drive
Bloomington, IN 47403
www.westbowpress.com
1-(866) 928-1240

Because of the dynamic nature of the Internet, any web addresses or links contained in this book may have changed since publication and may no longer be valid. The views expressed in this work are solely those of the author and do not necessarily reflect the views of the publisher, and the publisher hereby disclaims any responsibility for them.

Any people depicted in stock imagery provided by Thinkstock are models, and such images are being used for illustrative purposes only.

Certain stock imagery © Thinkstock.

ISBN: 978-1-4497-5698-7 (sc)
ISBN: 978-1-4497-5697-0 (e)

Library of Congress Control Number: 2012910965

Scripture quotations marked AKJV are taken from the American King James Version of the Bible.

Scripture quotations marked NASB are taken from the New American Standard Bible®, Copyright © 1960, 1962, 1963, 1968, 1971, 1972, 1973, 1975, 1977, 1995 by The Lockman Foundation. Used by permission." (www.Lockman.org)

Scripture quotations marked NIV are taken from the Holy Bible, New International Version®. Copyright © 1973, 1978, 1984 Biblica. Used by permission of Zondervan. All rights reserved.

Scripture quotations marked NLT are taken from the Holy Bible, New Living Translation, copyright 1996, 2004. Used by permission of Tyndale House Publishers, Inc., Wheaton, Illinois 60189. All rights reserved.

Scripture quotations marked TLB are taken from the Holy Bible, The Living Bible Translation, copyright 1974. Used by permission of Tyndale House Publishers, Inc., Wheaton, Illinois 60189. All rights reserved.

Printed in the United States of America

WestBow Press rev. date: 7/18/2012

For my husband, Russ, who always believes in me.
He has made everything beautiful in its time. (Ecclesiastes 3:11, NIV)

For our children, Jillian and Noah, who bring more to our
lives than we prayed or hoped.
*Now glory be to God who by his mighty power at work within
us is able to do far more than we would ever dare to ask or
even dream of — infinitely beyond our highest prayers, desires,
thoughts, or hopes.* (Ephesians 3:20, TLB)

In memory of my mentor, Rev. Otis Bell, whose prayers and
faith shaped my life.
Without faith, it is impossible to please God. (Hebrews 11:6, NIV)

Contents

Preface

Sometimes stories have to be told because of their potential to make the world a better place. Throughout Barb's battle with cancer (and it *was* a battle), I had the sense that the story should be shared. So many people struggle against cancer, and others strive to support those with the disease. I want to offer some hope and encouragement.

We had no special formula or ability to overcome this enemy. We did, however, find ourselves empowered by the prayers, love, and friendship of others. Only by the grace of God did we have the strength to persevere. Our faith became a vital, living force. My prayer is that good comes from relaying our experience with cancer.

For it is by grace you have been saved, through faith—and this is not from yourselves, it is the gift of God. (Ephesians 2:8, NIV)

Introduction

I am passionate about death! Walking with people "through the valley of the shadow" (Psalm 23:4, NIV) is the most rewarding aspect of pastoral ministry. Christianity teaches that victory over death is ours because of Jesus's resurrection. Journeying with people to the very edge of eternity inspires me like nothing else. Being in the presence of a person one second and knowing the next second that he or she is with the Lord stirs my soul.

One day, ministry to the suffering and dying became personal.

The voice I recognize as the Holy Spirit spoke to me four times between August 14 and 17, 2010. The message was the following: "Tragedy is coming to your extended family." On August 18, the call came from my niece. A tumor had been found near my sister's right pelvis.

Barb had stage-four cancer. She was fifty-two years old when the cancer was diagnosed in October 2010. Physicians at the Arthur G. James Cancer Hospital at Ohio State University predicted she had twelve to eighteen months to live at the time of diagnosis.

The cancer is called favour metastatic sarcoma. Tests indicated the cancer originated at another site; however, the scans, blood work, and biopsies never revealed the point of origin. No tumors were present besides the one on her right pelvic bone.

My congregation offers prayer concerns in worship every Sunday, and cancer patients are frequently mentioned. The disease is widespread. Seemingly everyone has a friend, neighbor, or relative battling this enemy. I would now like to share what I learned through this journey. My prayer is that the thoughts expressed here will bring readers encouragement, peace, and hope.

My sister was adamant that all those at her funeral be given the opportunity to invite Jesus Christ into their lives as Lord and Savior. The purpose of this book is to share the blessings that have come through this experience so that others will see the profound presence and involvement of the Lord as we journeyed "through the valley."

Nancy Goulet
February 2012

Chapter One

⟶

The Voice of God

My sister, Barb Ohlinger, had back pain and trouble walking since November 2008. X-rays were clear. No problems were detected, so she saw a chiropractor. Those treatments over a period of months didn't help. She occasionally felt some relief but frequently struggled to walk and cope with the pain.

Barb was preparing for her daughter Caroline's high school graduation party in May 2010 when she slipped on the wet floor. A few days later, she was on the back patio and fell again. Because she thought she had slipped on a wet leaf, she didn't relate either fall to anything but coincidences. No one dreamed of the mishaps and problems to come.

Barb limped at Caroline's graduation ceremony and began sleeping in the recliner to relieve the pain. By late July 2010, the torment was unbearable, and she had an emergency chiropractic visit. Again, scans revealed nothing. Chiropractic treatments continued. Though the sessions were guaranteed to be painless, Barb screamed in agony.

I wasn't seeking the Lord or even praying on August 14. It was a typical Saturday of housework. Cooking and cleaning were also on my mind, with a group from church expected the next afternoon. But while I wasn't talking to the Lord that day and the next three days, He was talking to me. I heard the Holy Spirit say, "Tragedy is coming to your extended family."

I questioned whether or not the voice was indeed God's. Why would God share such a message? What purpose was there in knowing this in advance? Does God reveal the future?

1

Other manifestations of the Holy Spirit have come in the previous several years. While I have served as a pastor, I have experienced the Holy Spirit's direction. These manifestations of the Holy Spirit were new for me. Nothing similar had occurred previously in my life. I neither sought them nor expected them, and on each occasion, I was surprised by God's movement.

Michele developed hydrocephalus as an adult. Shunts were inserted before her son's first birthday. Ten years later she had an MRI because the shunts were failing. I prayed with Michele in worship while offering anointing and healing prayer. A tingling sensation rose from the base of my spine to the top of my head. I received this as assurance from God that she was healed. She later confirmed the healing, stating, "All of a sudden everything was fine. The headaches and fogginess were gone. I went to the doctor that Monday and found out everything was working."

Another manifestation of the Spirit surprised me during an infant baptism. The air felt thick though not suffocating. I had never heard of such a thing but recognized this as the Holy Spirit's presence. When I shared the event with our bishop, Bruce Ough, he indicated he had experienced the same manifestation of the Holy Spirit in his life.

My church housed an adult day center, but the agency operating the facility announced plans to close that location. While in conversation with the registered nurse at the center, a channel of warm air burst from the ceiling and onto my face. I looked up. No furnace vents were visible. At that moment, I thought, *The church is to offer an adult day center to the community.* I received the burst of warm air as the Holy Spirit again sought my attention. The spirit of Jesus confirmed that the idea had come from above. Five years later, ADENA (Adult Day Enrichment of New Albany) is at capacity, and the ministry is thriving.

Francie Adams, director of ADENA, states that the Board of Directors desired individualized care plans for lower cognitive functioning Alzheimer's Disease patients. A special education teacher called to volunteer and provides this service. A social work student from Ohio State University heard about ADENA and accepted a salary at half the private-sector rate. Francie said, "We talk about something we'd like to add and God provides it immediately. It's exciting to come to work and see God moving. It's amazing to feel the Spirit work."

I recognized the Holy Spirit's words, "Tragedy is coming to your extended family," on August 14, 15, 16, and 17. The words were most certainly repeated so that I would get the message! I confess that it took me

2

that long to realize what was happening! There was no missing the message by the fourth time. The point was made. The revelation was heard. The voice I have come to recognize as the Lord's had spoken.

The next afternoon, August 18, Caroline called to say the chiropractor had sent them for scans because the procedure should not have caused any pain. A large tumor had been found near the right pelvic bone. I remembered the Holy Spirit's message and knew immediately that Barb was dying.

We searched for answers over the next six weeks. What was that monster? Could it be treated? The first cancer treatment center Barb visited turned her away with the earthshaking news that no one could handle her case. They knew from the X-rays that her tumor was beyond their area of expertise. And that meant more waiting.

We were fortunate to live near the Arthur G. James Cancer Hospital at Ohio State University. Even more amazing was the fact that Dr. Joel Mayerson was the only musculoskeletal oncologist in the Midwest, and he practiced at James! How horrible the trips to other states to see a specialist would have been. Barb was already struggling against unbearable pain. We were extremely blessed to have Barb under Dr. Mayerson's care.

Chapter Two

Her Life and Family

Barb was born March 29, 1958, in Norwalk, Ohio, the first daughter and third child of Leon and Pat Charville. Long black braids lie carefully wrapped in a cedar chest, a souvenir of her first haircut. She mastered clarinet and bells in the school concert and marching band, participated in the church youth group, sang alto in the youth choir, and was in Buttons and Bowls 4-H. She was an honor roll student and graduated fourth in her high school class.

One summer, Barb fell off a step and broke her foot. For several summers, she worked at Cedar Point, the amusement park in Sandusky, Ohio, which was only about ten miles from home. She snatched every offer for extended hours and good pay to sell glow-in-the-dark necklaces to park-goers after sundown.

She met Michael at a McDonald's on her lunch break from her first job at Harts in Columbus, and they married on July 19, 1986, in one hundred-degree heat. The church was not air-conditioned. We showered that morning only to become wet with perspiration immediately after we had dried.

Caroline Elizabeth Ohlinger was born by cesarean section on October 10, 1991. She arrived ten weeks early and weighed two pounds, two ounces. Barb had developed toxemia; her blood pressure elevated to stroke level, which was over two hundred. The baby had to be taken immediately. A nurse accompanied her from the doctor's office to the hospital because of the dangerously high blood pressure.

Barb and Michael wanted several children but knew her body could not tolerate another pregnancy. They decided she would stay home and raise Caroline, and Barb provided child care to other families in her home. Over the next nineteen years, Barb helped raise eighty-seven children. The household was run like a well-oiled machine, each child knowing and following the rules, one being that they line up from littlest to biggest when they wanted to swim in the backyard pool.

Barb would rather be outdoors than inside any day of the week. She walked outside barefoot, even in the snow. Parents dropped off children for child care and asked, "Are those bare footprints in the snow?"

Barb's life revolved around raising Caroline in a godly home. No one but God comprehended how limited those hours would be between mother and daughter. Most mothers work outside the home, requiring a few more years to log the time Barb and Caroline shared.

When he was twelve years old, Michael's son, Joshua, moved into their home, and Barb helped raise him. Barb loved him without hesitation, as though he were her own son. Josh wanted Barb to adopt him, but she and his dad explained how hurt his birth mother would feel.

Barb didn't like to swim alone, and it was always Josh who swam with her in their backyard pool. Josh helped paint the walls when she had a project. He made kitchen shelves in his high school shop class and performed maintenance on Barb's car. She planned and hosted Josh's high school graduation party. He and Barb had part-time jobs at Mama Linda's Pizza Shop in Pataskala, Ohio. He repaired her computer as needed, sometimes working until 11:00 p.m. She was the first person to offer help with his wedding. Josh feigned strength while Barb was ill, but when she died, he wanted time alone with her. He was torn up.

Weekends were divided between church and children's activities. Barb and Michael never missed one marching band half-time show, dance recital, *Cabaret* performance, or choir concert. *Cabaret* was shown three consecutive nights annually during their high school careers, and Barb enthusiastically attended each one!

One year, Michael and Barb celebrated their wedding anniversary at Cherry Valley Lodge in Newark. Before the last dinner course, Barb wanted the children to join them in swimming at the lodge. They talked on the phone that night "forever," and she missed them so much they drove home first thing in the morning! Barb and Michael did not normally go anywhere without the kids; they came along to the grocery store and on errands. If someone from church invited them to a get-together without the children, Barb and Michael shared why they chose not to attend.

Barb served for years as her church's director of children's ministries. She initiated many unique ministries, often with only the support of her family at the inception. The annual weeklong music camp brought together fifty-five community children; they had to turn some children away when capacity was reached. The campers learned and presented a musical to family and friends on Friday evening. Barb also launched the children's carnival, a six-week dance camp, and a children's choir.

She started adult ministries, including a women's book club, Oasis group for senior citizens, and other women's events. A Christmas gathering in December 2009 focused on the theme "Merry Mas: Putting Christ in Christmas."

A friend shared at the funeral how instrumental Barb was in motivating people to serve. She encouraged them to "step out of the box" and go where God was leading. Michael believes Barb was the shyest woman one would ever meet. One night, she sat on the bed crying, asking through the tears, "How can I get people involved?" He advised her to stop telephoning them and invite their involvement in person. She began asking them on Sunday mornings at church: "When are you going to sign up to help with music camp? Do you want me to get you the sign-up sheet?" Her words stretched them, and many did move beyond their comfort zones.

Time passed, and the pain developed. The illness was discovered, and it quickly worsened. Caroline started college, and Michael and Caroline needed help. They couldn't manage the twenty-four-hour care that Barb needed along with school and jobs. Michael asked his mother, Ginny, if she would move into their home to assist with Barb's care. Ginny was not physically strong after two heart attacks, open-heart surgery, and stint surgery the previous year; however, she moved in the day after she was asked to care for Barb, and she started to manage the household the morning after the diagnosis was received on October 8, 2010.

Ginny cooked, cleaned, did laundry, ran errands, and made countless trips to the pharmacy for bandages. Ginny cleaned up the "messy jobs" associated with the C. diff virus (clostridium difficile). She provided wound care; Barb's cancer ate through her skin and the exposed cancer required treatment several times daily. The seeping, decaying tumor fluids soaked bandages. She took over when the others could not stomach the mess. She packed their suitcases for the hospital stays and took food to the family who grew weary of hospital cuisine. Ginny was a gift from God, and her strong faith in Jesus Christ was apparent every day as she quietly, faithfully served.

The children for whom Barb provided child care frequently visited during her illness. How ironic that of the babysitting families who attended the visitation, the first was the first child she cared for, and the last was the final child she babysat.

When Michael and Barb's one-year-old granddaughter Jenna visited, she bypassed everyone and ran straight to Grandma. She called Barb "Ma-ga," which was "Grandma" backward! Jenna loved to sit on Ma-ga's lap for the reading of their favorite book, *The Hungry Caterpillar.* Barb recorded books for Jenna, and Jenna's favorites were always the "Ma-ga books." Barb knitted scarves for Caroline and Jenna, and one-year-old Jenna knew to wrap it around her neck! She still wants to wear it on every trip outdoors. When Jenna was born, Barb was the first to feed Jenna a bottle after Jenna's parents. She was the first relative to keep Jenna overnight. Their bond was tight; Jenna's visits brightened Barb's day like nothing else could. How difficult it was for Josh and Carrie when Barb was no longer able to provide child care.

Several months into her illness, Barb refused liquids—chocolate milk, white milk, Boost, root beer, water, popsicles, and Hawaiian Punch. Nothing sounded appetizing. Caroline's boyfriend, Rick, tried to get her to drink because Barb had a special connection with Rick. He asked, "Hey, Barb, what do you want to drink? Hawaiian Punch?"

She said, "Sure!"

Rick's mother died from cancer in December 2010, just seven months before Barb passed away. He understood the family's pain and was a gift to all.

Barb's hairstylist traveled to the house to cut her hair when illness prevented Barb from leaving home. After the discovery of the tumor in August, she only went to doctor visits, treatments, and the hospital. One Sunday morning, she was ready to have her hair cut short before hair loss began with the first round of chemo. She grieved as Michael shaved her head that morning. When hair loss began, she used a lint brush on her head daily to collect freshly loosened strands. Ladies from her church sewed head scarves to cover her baldness. Caroline got a blue highlight in her hair—blue represents bone cancer.

People were so very kind throughout this period in our life. Their neighbor, Bob, who was a dentist, provided free dental work to Barb and

Caroline. The staff at the Kroger pharmacy in Pataskala always let the family move to the front of the line when they stopped for her prescriptions.

Barb's world became increasingly small, limited to the living room with the hospital bed and commode, and the kitchen for a change of scenery. She ate meals at the kitchen table when she wasn't falling asleep in her plate. Jigsaw puzzles filled moments when she could focus. Six weeks before her death, she was anxious to finish a puzzle. As soon as the last piece was inserted, she called everyone to look. Then she immediately tore it apart and started assembling the next one in the pile. She was on a mission to complete them all before she died! After a time, chemo fog reigned, and she removed more pieces than she added. Exhaustion took over, and she only made it to the kitchen for a meal once weekly.

Barb managed alone at night for the first few months. If her leg fell out of bed, she called Michael or Caroline's cell phone and said, "My leg jumped!" She was unable to lift the leg herself. It had doubled in size because of fluid retention.

Months of caregiving takes a toll on the family. They took five-hour shifts at night, attempting to get a little rest. Caroline and Rick cared for Barb from midnight till 5:00 a.m. Michael was off work the last three months of Barb's life, and he took the 5:00 a.m. to 10:00 a.m. shift. They all helped throughout the day, including Michael's mom, Ginny. As Michael said at the time of Barb's death in July, "We won't be caught up on sleep until Christmas." Barb called Caroline's shift "sleepovers."

Because she had always been a chocolate lover, after Barb was told her diet could consist of anything that sounded good, her breakfast was comprised of chocolate milk and "donuts" (aka Hostess cupcakes)!

The combination of chemo fog and medication buffet and perhaps the movement of cancer to the brain as her life waned created confusion. One day, Barb thought a black child was seated on the end of her bed, but it was her dark blanket. My aunt vacuumed the ceiling for Barb where she saw spiders.

By this time, we were asking God to end her suffering.

Chapter Three

⁓

Fading Away

B arb asked me to visit so that we could discuss final conversations she wanted to have with her children. What should she say? What did they need from her at this point? When I arrived at her home on June 12, their well-being was the first topic on her agenda. She would tell them she loves them, she knows they'll be fine, they're wonderful people, she is proud of them and gave her life to raising them. She was weepy but matter-of-fact about the reality she faced. Clearly, prayers sustained her.

Barb reviewed her eulogy, and we discussed this book. I told her about a song I had recently heard on the radio called "Blessings" by Laura Story. The lyrics speak to Barb's situation, and she wanted to hear them. She viewed the song twice on YouTube and focused on the lyrics as they scrolled past.

I sensed she was in the process of coming to terms with her death. A few weeks later, Michael told their pastor that Barb had not entered the final stage prior to death. Barb opened her eyes and said, "Yes, I have."

Barb learned in May that she may live only days with an infection. Weeks later, the hospice staff wondered why she was holding on and fighting death so tenaciously. What was unfinished? Clearly, Barb had not come to the end of her agenda!

Our final Friday visit was July 15. Barb was groggy from the medication, and the cancer had possibly moved to her brain already. She was somewhat childlike when she spoke and easily moved to tears. The game show channel on television played across the room. Games passed the time over the sleepless months. She was getting answers correct up to three days before her death!

Attempting to make conversation, I said, "It's Friday, July 15."

She opened her eyes and cried, "Don't tell me that!" We wondered if she was trying to live until her twenty-fifth wedding anniversary on July 19, the following Tuesday. Had mention of the date told her how close she was to death? We cannot say for certain, but hindsight indicates so. At 5:45 a.m. on July 19, 2011, she passed into the arms of Jesus. Michael wished her, "Happy anniversary," and an hour later, she was gone.

Caroline held her mama's hand throughout the night while she talked to her. Barb sometimes squeezed her finger just a few hours before she died.

God was so very gracious to grant her heart's desire! Perhaps in the quiet hours over the months, she had prayed for that gift. Lingering until the anniversary meant more suffering, but with it, her dream came true!

Chapter Four

~~

E-Mail Journal of Barb's Illness

Sent: Wednesday, August 18, 2010, 6:16 p.m.

Subject: prayer request

Hi,

My sister, Barb, has had recurring back problems for over a year and was treated by a chiropractor. Today, he ordered an X-ray and discovered an "unfriendly" pelvic mass.

They are members of Etna UMC near Pataskala. She is a year older than me.

Your prayers are appreciated. Their daughter graduated in June.

Sent: Wednesday, August 25, 2010, 1:02 p.m.

Subject: Barb

Hi,

Hopefully, you received the mass e-mail sent last week on behalf of my sister, Barb, seeking prayer. With the length of time she's had pain, I think the outcome will be a sad one. It is a very uncertain time for our family. Barb is a year older than me, so she is still quite young, and a member at Etna United Methodist Church.

Sent: Thursday, September 16, 2010, 2:34 p.m.

Subject: Barb

Hi,

My family and I so much appreciate your prayers for my sister, Barb. It has been a month since the tumor was discovered.

She saw the specialist this morning at the James Cancer Hospital at Ohio State University to get test results. The pelvic tumor eating into the bone is not the primary cancer site. She is having a PET scan to find where else it is. It is not in the lungs and bones. Her only pain is in the pelvic area. The doctor will operate, and recovery will take a year; however, she will never be pain-free. It is better to wait for the PET results and know what he is dealing with before operating. We are thankful that the only specialist in the Midwest is at James.

We so appreciate your prayers. Their faith is very strong. Her pain is intense (screaming and crying) even with OxyContin and Vicodin. Pray for surgery to happen soon.

Thanks for being there.

Sent: Tuesday, September 21, 2010, 10:33 a.m.

Subject: RE: Barb

Good morning,

A quick note to say we received good news yesterday—the first. The needle biopsy had shown there was more cancer, but the PET scan indicates there is none! Answered prayer! A miracle! Tomorrow is a surgical biopsy to see exactly what they are dealing with. She returns to the doctor next week for results and then surgery lasting eight to ten hours. The doctor said the tumor is only three to six months old, so we don't yet know why pain started in November 2008.

Sent: Monday, October 04, 2010, 12:28 p.m.

Subject: diagnosis tomorrow

Barb gets her diagnosis and course of treatment tomorrow. A week ago Friday, her daughter, Caroline, soon to be nineteen, was hit by a drunk driver, spent a few days at Grant Hospital, and is recovering at home. She had to drop out of OSU for the quarter, and she'd only begun the week before. Michael missed work last week with knee trouble. He is in need of knee replacements, but he's too young for surgery because he won't be able to work again. Why is this family being hammered?

Wednesday will be seven weeks since the tumor was found, and *it is time* for some answers and progress. We feel the prayers of many holding us up. Barb's praise team from Etna UMC came over two weeks ago because she said on Facebook she was missing worship. Fifteen of them sang in their living room around her hospital bed for two hours. Very cool. There have been many complications and test delays and further tests ordered plus the fact that this doctor is in such demand, the only specialist in the Midwest for tumors growing into muscle and bone. I fully expect it to be stage-four. (Remember the Holy Spirit's messages from August 14 to 17: "Tragedy is coming to your family," and then there was the tumor discovery on the 18th.) I was glad when the doctor told Caroline to drop out this quarter—a great burden to start college and have her mom going through this. Their doctor visit is at 8:00 a.m.

Sent: Wednesday, October 06, 2010, 12:35 p.m.

Subject: Barb hospitalized

Hi,

My sister, Barb, was hospitalized at the James Cancer Hospital at OSU yesterday with an infection in the surgical biopsy wound. She will remain there until they receive the biopsy results; they have sent the sample to Johns Hopkins and Philadelphia for analysis. The concern is that one test—only one of many tests—indicates there may be cancer at another undetermined site. If that is the case, they will make her comfortable "until it is over" (Barb's words).

If that test comes back clear, she will have surgery next week, during which part of her pelvis and her right leg will be removed. The cancer can then be cured with chemo and radiation.

As you can tell, we don't have any certain answers yet, except that we know it is bone cancer (which explains the intense pain).

Thank you for your prayers and concern.

Sent: Thursday, October 07, 2010, 9:14 p.m.

Subject: Barb's diagnosis

Good evening,

Some of you received a portion of this via text messaging.

Tonight, we learned that my only sister, Barb Ohlinger, has a tumor attached to her right pelvic bone called metastatic sarcoma. While the doctors at OSU, Johns Hopkins, Stanford, and Philadelphia couldn't determine where the other cancer is, they at least know it is a form that spreads.

Surgery would mean losing her right leg, half the pelvis, urethra, etc., and she would have twelve to eighteen months to live. Without the surgery, she has twelve to eighteen months to live. There will be no surgery.

She wants to be home as much as she can, and they are beginning radiation or chemo soon to shrink it and reduce the pain. (She started a pain pump yesterday. The tumor is growing quickly.)

In a month, the pelvis will break due to the cancer eating it, and she will be hospitalized to deal with the pain.

Tomorrow at 7:30, they will perform surgery to wash out the infection. (Antibiotics aren't helping.) They didn't want to do this if she could survive because this causes the cancer to spread. Now they know they have nothing to lose. They sent a culture of the infection to Johns Hopkins for analysis. All they know for certain is that she has something very rare, apparently beyond identification.

Caroline turns nineteen on Sunday. Michael is telling her this news tonight. She continues to recover at home from the September 24 accident when she was hit by a drunk driver.

I am surprised Barb has twelve to eighteen months left. I have told Russ for the past seven weeks that she'll be gone by Christmas. (What do I know?) What is it with all the fifty-two-year-olds dying lately? *The Columbus Dispatch* seems to run several a week.

My brother from Raleigh is driving all night. My oldest brother from Atlanta is coming Saturday. The other two brothers are with my mom tonight. I am spending tomorrow at James.

Part of me is very envious of my sister. She gets to see Jesus soon! I am *so* ready to go. It's hard to be sad for her!

Thanks for your interest, prayers, and concern. I won't keep you posted as frequently. Let me know when you want an update.

I wish you were here now so that I could give you a big hug and express my love for you. Please learn from this. We are not promised tomorrow. Celebrate the temporary.

Sent: Thursday, October 28, 2010, 3:52 p.m.

Hi,

I could feel the prayers on October 6. Thanks for praying for my sister. The next day, we got the diagnosis. She is at James emergency room today; there may be an infection. They *really* need to start chemo next week. Praying it's not an infection. Flu would be better. The pelvis broke only a *week* after the doctor said it would break in a *month*. The cancer appears to be moving faster than he expected. I am going tomorrow.

But life is great. Wonderful family, fine congregation, prayers are buoying my hurting family over Barb's diagnosis. She calls the twelve-to-eighteen-month prognosis her "expiration date," not life expectancy.

Sent: Monday, November 08, 2010, 2:25 p.m.

Not visiting Barb today. She didn't have the flu. It is the C. diff virus due to all the antibiotics from the surgical biopsy infection. It is highly contagious, so this is a great day to work. The chemo was postponed. Do you know they can't start chemo with antibiotics in the system? Still no treatments to reduce the pain. Bummer. She is dying, and nothing is happening to help her, except *lots* of narcotics. I'm looking forward to visiting to check on her spirit. She has always been such a pleasant person. Don't want this to change her. She has been pretty subdued on the phone. (We talk daily.)

I appreciate this quote by Phillip Brooks:

> Do not pray for easy lives, *pray to be stronger people*; do not pray for tasks equal to your powers, *pray for powers equal to your tasks*. Then the doing of your work may be no miracle, but *you shall be a miracle*. Every day you shall *wonder* at yourself, *the richness of the life that has come to you by the grace of God*.

Hopefully, Barb is well enough to start chemo today. She is at the doctor's. I haven't heard.

My mom just called. They cannot start Barb's chemo today either. Maybe next week. That is discouraging news. They sent her for a Doppler ultrasound test on her leg. It is swelling due to the tumor, and they need to see what damage is being done. They ordered home health care to start tomorrow. It seems like she is going to die without any treatment at all.

Sent: Friday, November 12, 2010, 10:54 a.m.

Subject: change of plans

Good morning,

My brother Dave called to say that he and my mom will be here at 1:30 for me to drive them to the hospital to visit Barb. They don't know Columbus and prefer this to driving themselves.

Barb was rushed to the OSU emergency room on Tuesday night and finally got to a step-down unit at 5:30 a.m. on Wednesday. The

C. diff virus is back. She was hospitalized with it two weeks ago, but now she is very weak. Weakness is the reason they could not start chemo on Monday, and now it will be pushed even further back, if she ever gets it at all. She is very sick. C. diff is contagious, and we have not visited until now; however, she needs her family. Michael and Caroline have been with her the whole time. She is at James. The staff has been great with her, increasing her pain medications, explaining why they can't start chemo, etc.

It's more and more obvious that she is slipping away faster than the twelve to eighteen months the surgeon anticipated. Every time she is confused, I wonder if it is in her brain.

Sent: Thursday, December 02, 2010, 4:24 p.m.

Subject: update on Barb

Good afternoon,

Thank you for your concern for Barb. This is an update on her condition.

She had her first chemo on Monday the 22nd (it took all day), and immediately the pain left. What a blessing! Her pain has been horrible. She has not needed pain pills since chemo!

Monday, she had seepage from the biopsy wound. (It is an open wound.) Tuesday, we saw the surgeon, and he said the tumor may begin to grow out of the hole. (It is an inch inside). If it does, the tumor will become infected and bleed, and she'll bleed to death. Michael told me later they had heard that previously, but it hit Barb hard. When the doctor left the room, she said through her sobs, "I hope I live till Christmas."

Perhaps that won't happen. The chemo is helping, and the second treatment is December 13. (They are every three weeks, and after the third treatment, they will check for progress. Clearly, it has helped already.)

That was the first time I met Dr. Mayerson. Everything I heard about him was true. I wrote and thanked him yesterday for being gentle, direct, and compassionate with people amidst great sorrow.

Barb is no longer a candidate for surgery; therefore, his work with her ended Tuesday. She is now solely under the oncologist's care.

A few minutes ago, Barb sent a text asking when I can come over and plan her funeral. Michael is ready now. I imagine it will happen in the next day or two. I called her and she said, "We have to face what is coming." Then her home health nurse called, and she had to go.

This is something she put on Facebook:

> This is what I have been learning. If we slow down long enough to give *and* we slow down long enough to receive, life is amazing. There are people wanting to give and people needing to receive. When you get that right match together ... the outcome is unbelievable. Thank you, dear friends and family. Sept. 19.

Barb's best friend from church has told her she cannot take it anymore and has not been around for two months.

I hope you aren't wishing I hadn't written! You can see that the number of recipients has dwindled. Everybody deals with grief and loss in their own way. I understand that. This is what I know: There is beauty in every breath and heartbeat. The Lord is unwaveringly faithful to His children. Sometimes when we're "walking through the valley," it's actually a crawl, but with His help, we can keep moving.

This is for me a very privileged time. I have great joy and peace.

Sent: Thursday, December 9, 2010, 7:58:13 p.m.

Subject: tomorrow

Hi,

Last night before we started planning Barb's funeral, I told her my friend wants to visit, and I asked, "Is that okay?" She nodded and then asked why people she has never met are contacting her. I told her it's because she is inspiring and people want to be around folks like that. Michael mentioned Stephanie Spielman and Heather Pick as two others whose cancer inspired many.

They learned today she has C. diff virus again, and it is very contagious. None have caught it. Frequent hand-washing is the key. But a visit is entirely up to you.

Barb is declining quickly. It seems like the virus or poor nutrition will take her before the cancer does. Her appearance changed dramatically in a week's time. She is losing weight quickly and eating little. The blood work last week showed her nutrition is very poor.

I am just telling you that because with Christmas coming and all your commitments, I don't know how many more opportunities you'll have to visit. What I can say for certain is that unless the Lord intervenes in a way He hasn't done so far, she is in rapid decline.

The wonderful news is that yesterday the home health nurse measured the wound and said it is lots smaller than a week ago! Praise God! Answered prayer!

Sent: Wednesday, December 22, 2010, 10:40 a.m.

Subject: Update

Something miraculous is happening to Barb. Now that the C. diff virus has passed, she has become much stronger. She seems like herself again. Last night, her leg fell out of bed, and that brought considerable pain until someone got there to help. She has no control of her right leg now. It has swollen to about twice its usual size due to the tumor blocking circulation, and she still can't do anything for herself; however, her mind and faith are strong despite some "chemo fog." On the 10th, the palliative care nurse told me she would live till Christmas by sheer will, but she didn't know the effect the chemo would have when coupled with prayer!

Sent: Wednesday, January 26, 2011, 6:48 p.m.

Subject: Good news!

Hi,

I want to take advantage of the opportunity to share good news about Barb. Her radiation started last Friday, and the tumor shrank immediately! She saw the doctor on Monday, and he could tell a difference, too. Her leg, which is about double its normal size, is not nearly as firm as it had become lately. The Doctor indicated that fast-growing tumors respond well to radiation.

She is having daily radiation at 4:45. I take her on Fridays. She goes fifteen times and is then evaluated. How miraculous that this woman, who has not lain flat in a bed since May, is able with double the pain medication to have a daily five-minute radiation dose!

She got blue for the first time the week of January 4 when the home health nurse discovered the cancer had grown through the skin. She started a "happy pill" and is her cheerful self again. That cancer was growing quickly through the skin. The first time I saw it, the wound was about three inches by three inches. Two weeks later, it was about three inches by seven inches, sticking out about an inch farther, and her entire lower abdomen looked like it would pop with the pressure of the tumor. The radiation came just in time.

How can the human body function with an open wound? How does that work? It's fascinating.

The computer screen the radiologists were using appeared to reveal (to my untrained eye) that the tumor encompasses the entire pelvic area. Her radiation marks extend from one hip to the other.

Today Barb had surgery to receive her medi-port which will make the transfusions and chemo much easier.

I continue to recall Dr. Mayerson's warning that if the tumor grew through the skin it would begin to bleed and she would bleed to death. But for now, there are better days.

People say things like "I know what you're going through … I know how difficult this is." But it isn't difficult. So many, many people are praying, and the power behind those prayers is not only carrying us, but inspiring and invigorating us. Reflecting upon this yesterday, I wondered how people manage when others aren't praying for them. Who is overlooked? How are they coping? Prayer is more vital than I ever knew.

There is so much good in this. *Thank you* for your part in making this an enriching time.

Sent: Saturday, March 05, 2011, 4:21 p.m.

Barb's status changes weekly, but she is holding her own. They've asked the church for no more pot roast meals! Apparently, United Methodists love pot roast and wanted to share a nice meal!

Sent: Saturday, March 19, 2011, 6:47 p.m.

Subject: Barb

She was admitted to the James Cancer Hospital at OSU last night, where she will be for at least a week. She has a skin infection from the severe stretching in her leg due to lymphedema. They are also looking for a blood clot and are concerned about oxygen levels in the leg due to the swelling.

I was astonished upon arrival yesterday morning to see how much her already huge legs and waist had increased in a week's time. When she tried to lift herself off the commode, which is extremely difficult due to the weight of her abdomen and legs coupled with weakness, she lost her balance and fell forward onto the hospital bed. The massive size of her legs caused her to lose balance. Thankfully, she didn't fall another direction and hit the floor. She was unable to get up and was extremely frightened by the fall.

Barb and I left at 3:00 for her follow-up visit with the radiologist at James, and in the meantime, Caroline called the oncologist about getting a larger commode. The doctor was highly concerned about her legs. In the meantime, we discovered her temperature was 99 degrees when she was with Dr. Martin, the radiologist. As we were arriving at the car to transfer her from the wheelchair to drive home, Caroline called and said we were to go straight to the emergency room, where she would be admitted. She was a level-one priority due to the possible blood clot and fever, which was at 99.3 in the emergency room.

They confirmed the leg infection last night with her temp continuing to rise. Today brought a transfusion—she was a six, meaning in the danger zone. She had a CT scan, oxygen test, and the infectious disease doctors are consulting regarding her course of treatment.

Michael can't miss work this week because they are laying people off and he is concerned they may say he needs to be with his wife. Barb feels better when he is there at night, so we're working out visits. OSU is on spring break, so Caroline can be there a lot.

I was touched yesterday by Dr. Martin's compassion. He went into the radiation treatments knowing he couldn't cure her but believing her life would be much more comfortable. That hasn't happened because the tumor, as it continues to die, turns to a brothlike substance that is creating the lymphodema. She can't elevate her legs enough to flush it out due to the pain.

The current round of chemo is addressing the spots in her lungs. Monday's intense treatment was to address the hip pain, but that is cancelled due to the infection.

Yesterday, it was obvious that these treatments are not going to improve her quality of life. Michael says that because she is not herself anymore due to the medications, she is giving up. She doesn't have the fight in her that she used to have.

I praise the Lord for each moment we share and the opportunities to care for her.

I observe people at James and realize we are all thrust into a group that, six or twelve months ago, no one knew we'd be part of. For the many cheerful spirits we've encountered, the will to live that we observe so often, and the tender care of the medical community, I am truly grateful.

Barb's birthday is the 29th, and we've asked her church to give her a card shower.

Sent: Wednesday, March 23, 2011, 4:04 p.m.

Thanks for remembering Barb. Last week while driving to the radiologist, she said she is afraid.

I took my mom, aunt, and uncle down Monday afternoon, and Barb was so subdued. The medication must be causing that. My mom stood at the foot of the bed, looking at Barb with such an anguished expression. You and I have talked about how hard it is for a parent to lose a child. How much more can go wrong before death comes?

Sent: Wednesday, April 06, 2011, 7:48 p.m.

Subject: Race for the Cure

Hello,

Just want to let you know that Jillian and I are joining Barb's daughter, Caroline, in the Race for the Cure on Saturday the 16th in Springfield. Our shirts will be blue and silver (bone cancer colors) with Barb's name on the front and "Still fighting" on the back.

Bone cancer research doesn't have much money to work with since it is not a very common cancer. You may recall Barb's diagnosis last October was metastatic sarcoma, and while tests revealed it had metastasized, pathologists could not determine its point of origin. There are no other tumors. This makes her cancer even rarer.

Date: Monday, May 16, 2011, 1:04 p.m.

Subject: Barb may be dying

My brother Gene just called from Raleigh. Barb called him but couldn't talk, so Michael told him.

They are at the oncologist's office. The results came from the CT and bone scan I took Barb to on Friday. The lung spot is bigger. The other lung has spots now.

She has an infection in the tumor near the groin (I suppose the exposed cancer). It has entered her bloodstream, and she will be dead in two days. They could go home with hospice.

Or they could go to James and receive a drain tube and fight the infection with all their might and try to get her through it. If she survives—a big if—she has to decide if she wants more chemo (since it isn't stopping the spread).

Caroline called while Gene was on the phone. She is so very broken, only nineteen years old.

I'm trying to get things covered here so I can go to James.

The past two Fridays, the tumor and legs were so massive—the growth was so obvious—and we'd wondered how it could grow any bigger.

May 29, my nephew (Gene's son) is getting married in Boston. I'm officiating. A lot can happen between now and then.

Thanks for your friendship and prayer support.

Date: Friday, May 20, 2011, 11:29 p.m.

Subject: home till she passes

Friends,

Tonight at 5:00, Barb and Michael left the James Cancer Hospital so she can die at home. When the doctor asked yesterday if she was going home or staying there till the end, I knew the end is very near. This week's antibiotics brought pain relief. When we learned the infection hadn't entered her bloodstream, we had a glimmer of hope, but those kind souls at James can do nothing more. They drained a gazillion bags of the infected, dead tumor fluid out of her pelvic area, but the tumor continues to die and produce more infected fluid while simultaneously growing like wildfire. The antibiotics they pumped into her this week have her inflated like a balloon. I learned Tuesday from Michael that January 2, when the lung cancer was discovered, Dr. Lehman said she would live three to five months. Barb is right on schedule. Michael said hospice is lined up, but they may not need it for a week or two. I expect her to be gone before the annual conference. Nephew Brian's wedding is next Saturday in Boston. Pray that we don't have to make that trip with grieving hearts.

This has been a terrific week: blessed, joy-filled, affirming. Interwoven into the blessings, sorrow was lurking. Driving home on Wednesday, I had a conversation with my mom about how the time comes when the most loving thing is to pray that a loved one no longer has to suffer. Parents shouldn't have to lose children.

That is one of the crappiest things in life. Driving home from the hospital yesterday, she called, having just heard from Barb that she is going home to hospice care. More of a mother's tears over the phone.

This week, I got a letter from England. The circuit superintendent I knew the year I was a World Methodist Council Youth and Community volunteer has died. He was ninety-six. He and Joyce were very kind to me that year in England. They visited Ohio on an exchange, and we shared the pulpit one Sunday in Waterville in '89. For thirty years, I expected there to be no Christmas card. He was old when I knew him! I thought sixty-five was old when I was twenty-one! I hope this doesn't sound selfish, but I wish Barb could have had a few of those years.

It really is peculiar. I am preparing to officiate at my nephew's wedding and my sister's funeral at the same time. That is life! Beginnings and endings. Joy and sorrow.

Funny how life goes on. Tomorrow, Jillian has a singing and dancing audition for a summer musical at the Marion Palace Theatre. We're going to the Polaris Olive Garden tomorrow night for my birthday supper. (Tiramisu is calling!) Sunday is Jillian's confirmation and lunch with the grandparents to follow. Hopefully, there will be time to visit Barb briefly on Sunday evening. It's important that we all see her again. I've read of people who grieve and see the world passing by. They want to holler, "Don't you know my _____ died! Pay respects! Grieve with me! Sympathize!"

I've never had to watch someone close gradually slip away. My dad had a heart attack. Aunt Mabel is ninety and was hospitalized this week because her pulse is now thirty! (Talk about a saint!) But her spirit is the same as always. I love walking with people to the edge of eternity. *Thank you* for your part in making these hallowed days through your loving support of our family.

Still hoping there is opportunity to talk with Barb about heaven and the book I'm writing.

Below is the church newsletter article written tonight about Barb. Perhaps I'll read it in the a.m. and decide it's more cathartic than helpful and won't use it! Tonight, it works.

Home-Going—As I write these words, it is May 20, and my sister is going home for the last time. Tonight, she was discharged from the James Cancer Hospital at OSU, and her husband is now driving her home. That is where she will stay until she passes away. That home-going—to her heavenly home—will be spectacular! By the time you receive this, she may have left us.

She was never able to visit our new home in Marion. Back trouble in July was diagnosed as cancer in August, and the disease took her strength from that time. Someday, her husband, Michael, and daughter, Caroline, will visit. Caroline will sing in worship, and you will be blessed! Until that day comes, please pray that healing comes to their home and they adjust to their new life without their wife and mother.

How must it feel to know one is making the last trip home? What thoughts must fill the mind of one who knows the days remaining could be counted on one hand? How does one prepare for a home-going?

The reality is that we prepare each day as "In Him, we live and move and have our being" (Acts 17:28, NIV) Life is preparation for our home-going if we deliberately live for Jesus. Is your faith intentional? Does it dictate your every move? Is your faith living and vital and growing? Is our resurrected Savior the center of your life? Do you live for Him? If so, home-going is a transition to a new way of living. It is not the end but a beautiful beginning.

This is my prayer for you. May you, in the time you have, prepare daily for your home-going so that when the time comes, the transition is beautiful. We are not promised tomorrow. Let's live each day for Jesus.

When we were in high school, Barb told me she didn't like it when the pastor repeated himself. Apparently, truth could only be mentioned once. Then it was time for another topic! I think of that sometimes when I pray in worship. There are phrases I like to use about representing Jesus, committing someone to God's tender, loving care, others I can't recall because I'm crashing. There is a song (whose sentiment at least) I'll refer to often. It's on 104.9 *The River* a lot, or you can hear it on YouTube. I've sung it (to myself) often this week. May it bless you as well. It is "Blessings" by Laura Story.

At the end of the day, I praise God for the privilege of these past few months with Barb. Your prayerful support has taken me deeper in the Lord than ever. Thank you for the blessing you are!

Sent: Thursday, June 02, 2011, 10:38 a.m.

Subject: photo

Good morning,

This photo, taken Monday, gives you an idea of how massive Barb's tumor has become. (There is sadness in Michael's eyes that I haven't seen until now.)

MEMORIAL DAY 2011

She is having tremendous pain, as you can see by the way she is sitting. Notice the calluses on her knuckles from pushing up to relieve the pain. She isn't able to sleep due to extreme agony. The hospice nurses can't control it, so a hospice doctor visited yesterday.

She is still eating well. Taking her favorite, apple pie, tomorrow.

She wrote this on Facebook Saturday night: "For those of you who haven't heard … I had to make a choice between quality of life and quantity of life. I chose quality. Hospice began visits this past week. Stopped chemo and letting the body work on its own … keep the prayers going please!" May 28 at 11:45 p.m.

At any time she could have a blood clot or heart attack since her system is under so much pressure. Her doctor told us at James (May 19) that if he were to take one of her pain pills, it would knock him over, but she has built up a tolerance to them over time. He then said narcotics are a gift from God for times like this and that sometimes the body does better without chemo at this point.

Caroline's OSU Newark professors got together and told her on the 23rd not to come to class anymore. They are sending her assignments via e-mail. How very kind.

We are the recipients of such grace. The Lord is so very faithful, and countless people are supportive, prayerful, loving, and kind. What a great combination! Such good comes from times such as this. You mean so much to us. Thank you!

Sent: Saturday, July 02, 2011, 8:07:14 p.m.

Subject: FW: Hello there!

Hello,

My friend Anne in England asked about Barb tonight, and I just sent her this update:

> Barb had the most pain ever last night. She screamed from 12:00 to 4:00 a.m. They spoke with the hospice nurse twice for an hour. The Doctor increased the oxycodone and methadone. Then the nurse showed up at 3:00 a.m. She took a turn for the worse today. She is too weak to move herself to the commode. She can't hold her water. Mainly sleeps. The hospice nurse said she has entered the end phase. I am going tomorrow after church, will be there by 3:00, and stay through Independence Day, if not longer. They need help. They haven't slept in weeks. She

sleeps in the recliner, leaning forward with her head on stacked pillows. She is so exhausted. She said last night she wants to die.

Caroline and Michael are really struggling.

Thank you for your prayers and support.

Sent: Monday, July 04, 2011, 11:44 p.m.

Subject: hospice assessment

Hello,

This is what Michael reported after the hospice assessment tonight: She is clearly fighting death. What is unfinished? Their twenty-fifth anniversary is the 19th. Don't be surprised if she dies on the 20th or 21st.

Barb is now permanently confined to bed with a catheter. Due to the location of her wounds, the catheter may need to be reinserted at 3:00 a.m.

Do not force foods. Encourage liquids.

Will have a liquid oxycodone for times her pain may become severe, like it was Friday night.

Despite all the movement and work on her body tonight, she settled right down after anxiety medicine. This indicates she is not in pain as much as was thought; it is anxiety, and the medication will be adjusted.

She has a couple end-of-life signs but not the imminent ones: dark urine; knees, joints, elbows discolored; can't wake her; nausea.

We'll see dramatic decline in her health. Already have. But it will be lots worse.

The nurse is happy with the care she is receiving.

She is lying flatter than she has been in months and is comfortable with it. They will try to gradually make her flatter and ease pressure on the hip.

Also, they will use the Kirkersville funeral home with visitation and the funeral at the church.

The cancer is not likely in the brain yet since the scan six weeks ago showed no signs of it there. Her confusion is due to medication.

On Jul 19, 2011, at 10:40 a.m., Nancy Goulet wrote:

Good morning,

Barb passed away at 5:45 a.m.

She entered the final stage Saturday at midnight. The nurse saw her yesterday and said she might last a few days. I was there from 5:00 to 10:00 p.m. She couldn't wake up but mouthed responses. "I love you, too."

Caroline and Rick had the night shift. (Rick's mom died of cancer in December.) They knew the end was coming and got Michael up at 5:00. Her breathing was very labored, and her heart was racing, pounding. Suddenly, at 5:45, it all stopped. She must have had a heart attack to stop so suddenly (my theory).

Finally, she is at rest. Praise be to God for the gift of *eternal* life.

Dad, brothers, and sister with Barb (standing), 1963.

Barb (middle right) with siblings, cousins, and grandparents, March 1967.

Barb, Michael, and Josh.

Caroline with her parents

Josh, Michael, Barb, Carrie, Ginny, Jenna and Caroline, Spring 2010.

Granddaughter Jenna with Ma-Ga and Papa.

Caroline and her Mama.

Stepfather Dick, Mom, Barb, and Caroline, December 2010.

During one of our December 2010 Friday visits.

Chapter Five

The Blessings of Prayer

When my son, Noah, was twenty-one months old, he was learning to pray. Several times during a meal, he would hold out his hands and say, "*Pair!*" We put down our forks and said a *pair*. Never mind that the next minute, he threw his plate across the room! Truly … he had quite a pitching arm! We thanked the Lord for splat mats!

How similar we are to twenty-one-month-olds. We sincerely pray with every fiber of our being. To the depth that we can understand moving the hands of the God of the universe through prayer, we pray. And sometimes, a minute later, we are throwing tantrums or throwing our weight around or throwing verbal punches.

Still, we pray. God, who made us, knows where we still need to grow and doesn't hold our shortcomings against us. Our foundation is prayer.

What is prayer? It is an admission that God is in control of our lives. It is two-way communication between the Creator and the creation. It is conversation with the Savior. It is a relationship-builder, a faith-enhancer, a hope-refiner.

God is not our errand boy. Approaching prayer as if we serve a "Gimme God" is self-centered rather than Christ-centered. The Lord often answers our prayers beyond our fondest imaginings, but God wants us to be open to His will and desires and the splendor He has for us.

My mentor, Otis Bell, was a United Methodist missionary in Japan and Okinawa for twenty years. He returned to the East Ohio Conference and was appointed to my home church, Edison Memorial United Methodist, when I was sixteen. He left after three years to become the conference evangelist. Six months later, he had a massive heart attack and went on disability leave. I prayed for God to heal his heart, but Otis said, "The healing has already been. I'm alive."

God always hears our prayers. He doesn't hear us selectively based upon the degree of devotion or commitment. God always works His will in His way. My mentor's heart was never healed, but the Lord gave him twenty-three more years to praise Him with a "broken," battered heart. Amazing! I want my life to sing God's praise when His answers are unexpected. Father knows best!

Otis taught me that death is not to be feared, and now journeying with someone to the edge of eternity is one of life's highest honors. Traveling the cancer road was nothing new to me, but no close relative had died of cancer, so this was different.

Barb texted me for the last time on June 12. She asked that I bring the funeral materials for her to review. That was the day I sought her permission to write this book. She was humbled and moved, desiring for many to hear how God was working through her illness. People prayed, cared, helped, and loved, bringing us all a little closer to God's purpose for our lives.

Caroline sang a solo during worship at my church in May 2010. She would graduate from high school in two weeks. The solo was beautiful and long overdue since we had talked about her singing in worship for years. Her dad was struck by the sermon theme, "The Giants We Face" from Numbers 13, the account of the spies investigating the Promised Land. Michael said their pastor recently had an eight- or nine-message series on giants; then they came to my church and heard the identical theme. Inside, I wondered if God were sending them a message.

I reminded Barb and Michael of that "coincidence" as we talked that June evening. Michael said he hadn't put it together, but yes, God was apparently preparing them for the giant coming their way. Hindsight sharpens acuity. God speaks, and when we are receptive to His message, He prepares us to face our giants.

Hearing the word from the Holy Spirit that our family would face tragedy didn't stop prayers for Barb's healing. Early on, I prayed for healing in case the spirit of God had not really spoken. Later, the prayers changed to cessation of pain and anxiety, and she could rest. Just as God told Joshua to be strong and courageous when facing the enemy (Joshua 1:6), that is my consistent prayer for people confronting the cancer enemy.

Sleep eluded Barb almost entirely from May to October 2010 because of her pain. Sometimes Barb would drop off to sleep while she was typing an e-mail, and we found lines of qqqqqqqqqqqqqqqqqqqqqqqqqqqqqqq down the page. She slept a moment or two until the pain returned. She tried to rest in the La-Z-Boy and longed to sleep in her bed again.

Sometimes when she didn't want us to hear her scream in pain, she rolled her wheelchair down the hall to the bedroom, leaned her head onto the bed, and cried out with every ounce of energy she possessed. How excruciating to realize that every hour of every day, she suffered. Her pain did not cease when I walked out her door every Friday afternoon. She struggled every minute of every day to move, to sleep, to urinate, to live. God gave her supernatural strength to endure the heartache and helplessness.

The power of prayer was nearly palpable. We felt uplifted through Barb's illness by the prayers of friends and family around the country. People said things like, "We know what you're going through. We know how hard this is," but it wasn't difficult! We were carried throughout the cancer journey by the prayers of countless believers.

This has to be why God, who is love, permits the evil of cancer. Good comes from it! People who perhaps otherwise would not pray start praying. Sometimes life brings experiences which cannot be handled with our limited human strength. We seek power beyond ourselves, and that power comes when we turn to God in prayer. Faith grows as thoughts very naturally turn to the purpose and brevity of life. As spiritual beings, we understandably consider our own mortality. People do make commitments to the Lord when they are facing a loved one's illness and death.

God created us to love Him and center our lives around his Son, Jesus Christ. He desires that our faith grow continually throughout our lifetime. The Holy Spirit works within us to create a loving, trusting relationship. When tragedy comes—and it *will* come—we are prepared because we stand on the firm foundation of faith. We learn to trust in the sunshine so we remain strong through the storm.

Barb and Michael's faith has always been life-sustaining. When Caroline's health was in a precarious place as an infant, they trusted. Michael said throughout Barb's illness that they trusted God's plan. The teaching they received while they were growing up in the church prepared them for life-threatening challenges.

So many times we visited their home during Barb's illness and left feeling uplifted. Joy and laughter filled the house because nothing can separate us from the love of the Lord (Romans 8:38–9). The joy of the Lord *was* their strength (Nehemiah 8:10). Michael said that is how their relationship was; they made fun of each other. Nothing bothered either of them.

Prayer buoyed their spirits and sustained them at an otherworldly level. They had the "peace of God which passes all understanding" (Philippians 4:7, AKJV). Prayer allowed them to *receive* what was happening with the confidence that "all things work together for good to them that love God" (Romans 8:28, AKJV).

So much of how one manages a terminal illness depends upon how the diagnosis is received. Does one receive it with confidence that the good Lord is "a very present help in trouble" (Psalm 46:1, NASB)? Does one believe that God, who is love, controls all that comes along? If so, one lives at peace with the realization that doctors find what the Lord *allows* them to find. Build the relationship when the sun shines so that the storm is received with peace.

God allows physicians to discover our health issues, and then He partners with us if we are willing. God comes alongside as comforter and helper to encourage and sustain (John 14:16). The Lord does not *send* illness; God is love, and there is nothing loving about orchestrating cancer. The Lord *permits* illness, heartache, and struggle to enter our lives with the comforting presence of the Holy Spirit, our sustainer.

If this sounds out-of-this-world, it should. God is ready to share Himself with us. The connection is strengthened through prayer and Bible study because God desires a relationship with us. We speak to Him in prayer; He speaks through His word. When we quiet ourselves before Him, He communicates His intentions and directions.

When we are praying for an ill loved one, God's will is always sought. His plan may not include physical healing, but relationships, spirits, hearts, and minds may be restored as God's spirit gently and lovingly moves and blesses.

The evening in October 2010 when Barb's diagnosis was finally known, there were lots of tears and great disappointment. The hoping and praying met the harsh reality of a stage-four cancer diagnosis. Prayer did not prevent sorrow. Theirs was not a carefree acceptance without question or doubt. Barb and Michael experienced the usual stages of grief. They were sustained through very real, raw, natural human reactions by the comforting presence of the Holy Spirit and the faithful prayers of God's people.

Barb longed for God to use her illness to draw people to Him. She wanted "everyone to get along" and find salvation in Jesus Christ. Her prayer for us was that her funeral service includes the opportunity for everyone present to repent and invite Christ into their lives as their savior. She sent this e-mail shortly after the tumor was discovered:

Sent: Monday, August 30, 2010, 12:11:26 p.m.

When I die ... not that I am expecting it to happen this go 'round, this is what I would like—I'm only telling you now so you can start practicing it at other funerals and have it perfected. At the end of the service, I want you to get everyone up to the altar somehow. In groups. Start with those who want to be saved ... then as a group or in sections, get everyone up there who has been saved. That leaves the ones sitting in the pew who haven't. Then address them pretty strongly, please, until everyone there has made their decision.

It was a powerful moment when nearly everyone present at her funeral service knelt at the altar to commit or recommit their lives to Jesus Christ. The music playing was, per Barb's instruction, "Defining Moment" by Newsong.

The prayers of hundreds of faithful friends over months and miles culminated in that moment when people poured from their seats. Barb's prayers were answered as commitments were made and hearts renewed. Her longing for others to know Jesus came to fruition in that moment.

Blessings and the accompanying peace were possible because of the prayers of many faithful people, some of whom never met Barb. God used their prayers in powerful ways. People truly partnered with the Holy Spirit in ministering to Barb through their prayers. What a blessing to know God listens to us and moves in the lives of others because we care enough to pray.

The questions that frequently came to my mind during Barb's illness included the following: *What about those for whom no one prays? How do they cope with cancer? Where do they find strength to fight the battle?* When we pray for people, they find needed strength and help.

When George Howard was director of the Conference Council on Ministries for the West Ohio Conference of the United Methodist Church, he said the fastest growing churches in the conference without exception were those with dynamic prayer ministries. They do nothing without first bathing the vision in prayer.

What could happen in our communities if the Christians began to pray for individuals and families with the same motivation? How might the ill be strengthened and healed emotionally, physically, and spiritually? How many broken families would be reunited? We would never know—not until we reach heaven—the number of addictions overcome, marriages restored, and souls saved because of our prayers.

A friend is currently struggling with liver cancer. He told the pastor of a Hispanic congregation that asked to pray with him. The prayer wasn't the typically brief one- or two-minute prayer. It was twenty minutes of fervent prayer that was more like worship. What if we all prayed with that intensity? How would we move the hands of God?

The culture tries to convince us that this life is all that matters. Our society very subtly works to absorb us into its image. God's word says, "Do not be conformed to this world, but be transformed" (Romans 12:2, NASB). The Christian's challenge is always to take a path contrary to the world's trail.

Our prayer lives and our faith in general are being held captive by our culture. We fill our days with modern conveniences, hobbies, obligations, errands, and interests. If there is any time remaining, God might get our leftovers as an afterthought. We think this is acceptable because it is the common American practice; all the while, Satan has us just where he wants us. We are less useful to God than we can and should be, and we don't even realize. The culture distracts us from the call to devoted, holy living, and Satan is delighted; meanwhile, prayers go unprayed.

Nevertheless, God is faithful and hears our prayers, however infrequent. How exciting to be part of this divine movement called prayer! God wants to reveal His love, power, and goodness in response to our prayers.

I arrived at church at 7:00 a.m. on Sunday, October 2, 2011. While I reflected on the morning to come, I felt the burden of responsibility of pastoral ministry. Colleagues speak of keeping tight control of their Sunday morning routines and not discussing any business so their minds are filled with prayer and the morning message before worship can begin. The need to remain focused on God before we proclaim the word is intense.

That morning, I especially felt the weight of responsibility for caring for the flock, so I prayed. The exact petition escapes me, but it was something like the following: "I cannot get through this on my own strength." At that exact moment, "heaven came down." There was a song in the '60s titled

"Heaven Came Down and Glory Filled My Soul" by John W. Peterson. Glory with a capital "G" filled me!

All morning, I loved the people more intensely than ever. *I truly loved them.* I felt like I was walking two feet off the ground. Nothing bothered me. It was *otherworldly*. I kept thinking, *This is what heaven feels like.* I asked the Holy Spirit to make it last, but after worship, the feeling gradually faded and was gone by 2:00 p.m. Now I have a clearer understanding of heaven. It was wonderful! Heaven came down!

If I could only capture the glory, much like the Israelites in their morning manna gathering (Exodus 16:17)! But it wasn't to be. Blessings are fresh each morning (Lamentations 3:22–3), not always in as profound a way as on October 2, but the blessings are there. The needs are met. God is faithful. St. Paul says, "Let heaven fill your thoughts" (Colossians 3:2, TLB). When you do, you will live expectantly.

Yet, sometimes despite our heartfelt, sincere prayers for healing, death comes. We do not understand why God chooses to physically heal some and others are destined to suffer and die. Barb suffered immensely. Her cancer grew through the skin, and the family treated the wound several times daily over the final seven months of her life. The funeral director said he had never seen anyone suffer as much as she suffered. Coupled with the exposed cancer was the horrific pain, which was part of cancer growing into a bone. Barb's knuckles bore calluses from months of lifting weight off her pelvis to reduce pain. Prayers did not stop the pain. My sister screamed and cried and suffered terribly. She took 1500 milligrams of oxycodone daily. This was the absolute highest dose tolerable, yet her pain was often uncontrolled. Morphine could not lessen the discomfort near the end, and gabapentin, methadone, prednisone, and dexamethasone were prescribed.

Jesus suffered in this life, and so shall we (2 Timothy 3:12). Why had Barb's suffering been so extreme? We have no idea. I cannot tell you God will remove your pain. He *will* remain a faithful, loving presence in the valley. Pray for eyes to see the ways God is healing. Pray for that healing to take the form God desires. Release your expectations. Pray for everyone who comes to mind. The Holy Spirit brings them to mind so that you will pray.

So shut the door and turn off the television, computer, anything that is noisy. You might want to light a candle, plug in a fountain, or do whatever creates that "prayer closet" for you. This place could be a desk where you leave your Bible and a notebook that's ready for use. Create peaceful surroundings and welcome the God of peace.

Peace came during a conversation three months before Barb died. My bishop asked how Barb was doing in April 2011, six months after her diagnosis. Following a brief update, he responded by saying, "It doesn't appear that God is going to heal her cancer."

His observation was very freeing. It was as though permission were given to view her illness from another perspective. Rather than longing and begging for healing, the time had come to prepare for the inevitable. Prayers changed from pleading for healing to requests for Barb to settle in and pass peacefully.

We humans think in terms of this life as the pinnacle. We cherish this life, and well we should. It is a gift. But the tendency is to cling to this life and not long for the next. Death is more easily accepted when our time on earth is viewed as preparation for the next life. Do you long for heaven? Do you have as little desire for this world as a dead person does? (Colossians 3:2, TLB) Do you "let heaven fill your thoughts" (Colossians 3:2, TLB)?

The new focus permitted any anxiety over unanswered prayer to give way to acceptance of God's will. Actually, our prayers *were* answered. Barb *was* healed. Death is the greatest healing possible. *God gave Barb His best!*

My bishop's observation brought peace. It was as though I had permission to admit what I'd known since that August 2010 weekend. Tragedy had come to my extended family. *And in the tragedy, Barb received God's best.*

Let's linger here a moment. God gave Barb His best. *Recognizing* God's best in the midst of tragedy is the challenge. Join me in praying:

> Give us eyes, dear God, to see your answers!
>
> Give us faith, Loving Father, to trust when your ways are not our own!
>
> Give us strength, Precious Lord, when you give our loved ones your best! Amen.

Chapter Six

～

Headed Home to Heaven

Swinging in the backyard on a beautiful 75 degree day with a nice cup of tea caused me to exclaim to my young children, "This is really living!" We attempted to instill in them an appreciation for life and God's creation.

My four-year-old, Noah, was especially receptive. He noticed a glorious sunset beyond the windowed dining area and exclaimed, "Everyone come and see the sunset! This is really living!" We would lie on the grass in the backyard and watch the clouds dance by, and he would cheer, "This is really living!"

He "camped out" in the basement on Saturday night with his dad and sister so that I could have a good night's sleep before Sunday worship services. While he was drifting off to sleep, Noah often reminded me, "This is really living!"

I responded, "Noah, life doesn't get any better than this!" In many ways, it's true. With family, a sense of love and security, appreciation for God's blessings, peace with oneself, life doesn't get any better than this!

But it does! Scripture teaches that "no eye has seen, no ear has heard, no mind has conceived, what God has prepared for those who love him!" (1 Corinthians 2:9, NIV)

Life is better in heaven!

Early Christians anticipated the Lord's return in their lifetime. They lived expectantly on tiptoes. They longed for heaven and to be forever with the Lord. Over time, we have lost the longing. It has been replaced by self-satisfaction and ladder-climbing. We have forgotten why we are here. We are on the planet to serve our loving God as followers of Jesus. As we learn of Him and live for Him, we long to be with Him.

When my daughter, Jillian, was three years old, *The Wizard of Oz* was never far from our thoughts. She pretended to be Dorothy and viewed the movie daily for over four months! We would see people at the store or church, and Jillian would whisper, "Tell them I'm Dorothy!" Over those months, with great regularity, Russ was the wizard, Noah was a munchkin, and I was the wicked witch!

Because I have viewed the movie countless times, the image that lingers is not the munchkins, not the flying monkeys, not the medicine man behind the control booth curtain. The scene that replays in my mind is Dorothy struggling to open the storm cellar door. Inside is home. Auntie Em and Uncle Henry are there. Outside, the storm approaches.

That is so "lifelike!" If only we could get inside the storm cellar, if we could only make it home, we would be safe. In the meantime, we're pulling at the door, begging God to deliver us.

Jesus spoke of that home: "Let not your hearts be troubled" (John 14:1, TLB). He was saying if your heart is troubled in this world, you're focusing on the wrong thing. Focus your attention on heaven. Believe with all your heart that He is preparing your home. Think about heaven. Pray about heaven, long for heaven, but don't be troubled. Focus on the *next* life. Don't be tripped up by this one. Jesus said, "My Kingdom is not of this world" (John 18:36, TLB), and your home isn't either.

My mentor taught me that heaven isn't an extension of earth. There is such wonder and beauty that we can't imagine. He also said we must celebrate the temporary. Everything in life is temporary. The people we love aren't here forever. The experiences we share are meant to be treasured because yesterday is gone. Tomorrows don't always come, and each day is a gift.

He taught that heaven is not some faraway place. It is here, all around us, very near. We just can't see it. There are times when the presence of a deceased loved one can be sensed. Those moments cannot be forced; they are unpredictable.

Fourteen months after my father passed away, my mother moved into her dream house, a newly constructed home next door to the homestead. Thanksgiving was celebrated in the recently finished abode shortly after the move. I thought of my dad, and I wondered how he would feel about all the changes. My teenage nephews were playing a boisterous game of table tennis in the basement. I went downstairs to watch, and I saw my father standing next to the stairwell. He appeared to be about thirty years of age, thin, handsome, healthy, and laughing out loud at his grandson's antics! The privilege of seeing into the unseen world around us lasted only a second or two, and I witnessed him no more. But in that moment, an unforgettable gift was given.

Some people are suspicious of such occurrences and do not believe these things can happen. For them, it probably won't. If one is open to learning about and experiencing glimpses of the unseen activity around us, such visions are possible. If unable to see a loved one, his or her presence may be felt at times.

My mentor passed away in April 2002. My birthday fell the following month. While I was talking with my husband in the kitchen before supper one day, I felt a tingle rise up my spine, and I immediately thought, *Otis is wishing me a happy birthday!* Russ and I were astounded that the sensation came during an unrelated conversation. The event was unexpected, surprising, and unsought. Such "greetings" were previously unheard of by me; the notion that this was possible had never entered my mind.

The following winter, an ultrasound was required. While I was lying on the cot and waiting on the technician to determine if the scan was adequate, fear gripped me. What if I had cancer? My children were five and two years old; I couldn't leave them! Tears flowed from the depths of my being, and for the first time since his death, I talked to my mentor.

He was a godsend when he became pastor of our church. I was sixteen years old. He taught me about ministry and a faithful walk with Jesus throughout high school and college. When he died at age eighty-four, we had known each other for nearly twenty-seven years. I am the pastor and Christian I am due to his example, witness, and acceptance. He was supportive through every challenge and victory in life. Calling on him during that uncertain time was as natural as breathing.

The response was immediate. As I lay there, hands clasped under my head, I felt his physical presence on my right side, as if he was giving me a reassuring hug. That indication of his supportive presence was unexpected. Awe filled my being over the realization that our loved ones are very nearby and can continue a supportive ministry of presence even after death.

Labor Day weekend in 2008 while I was singing the Doxology in worship, I thought of Otis praising "Him above, ye heavenly host." Not only the angels were praising the Lord in heaven, but my friend was too! In my thoughts, I said to him, "I wish you were here to listen to my sermon," and he immediately said, "I am!"

These reassurances have come quite spontaneously. They have greatly enhanced my understanding of the next life. Like answered prayer, they do not always come when requested, and they always take a surprising form.

When my son was four years old, my husband and I were talking in the kitchen about a friend's recent massive heart attack and death. My little guy overheard the conversation, entered the room, and inquired, "Is he stuck in heaven?" One can be stuck in addiction, a bad marriage, or depression, but stuck in heaven? Obviously, that is how a four year-old mind processes the fact that when people die, we no longer see or hear from them. They are stuck!

Yes, the saints are beyond view, but they appear to be, at least occasionally, close enough to make contact. God didn't deliberately keep details about heaven from us to trouble us. That is not loving, and God is love. A more plausible explanation is that the grandeur of our heavenly home cannot be expressed in human-size thoughts.

What do we know about heaven?

1. We are with our Savior Jesus Christ in heaven (2 Corinthians 5:8; Philippians 1:23; Luke 23:43). Nothing surpasses spending eternity with the one who died to save our souls.

2. Heaven is a place of love, peace and rest, no regrets, no sin. Doesn't rest sound great? Ah!

3. Heaven is a place of reunion. We'll see loved ones, the saints who've gone before us. Hebrews 12:1 says these souls comprise the great cloud of witnesses who cheer us on. Remember that when life is tough or you feel alone. We will see family and friends who gave their lives to Jesus and lived for Him. Children will see grandparents. Spouses will be reunited, and parents will meet miscarried children for the first time.

4. We will be perfect in heaven—and your spouse has wanted perfection from you for a long time!

5. I believe we will feel completely understood. No one understands the creation like the Creator.

6. We don't know exactly where heaven is, but we do know that no one ever dies alone. The spirit of Christ is there, escorting us home.

7. There is no more hunger, death, crying, or pain in heaven (Revelation 21:4). The world's heartache is left behind like an old coat.

8. Our spirits are made to last forever; these bodies are not. Scripture teaches, "If the earthly tent we live in is destroyed, we have a building from God, an eternal house in heaven, not built by human hands" (2 Corinthians 5:1, NIV).

God has created us with a longing to be home, so let's stop the tugging between two worlds. Let's settle it once and for all and anticipate heaven as we serve God through His Son, Jesus Christ!

Chapter Seven

Coming to Terms

After our beloved dog, Abby, died in January 2004, we all wanted another dog. We tried a Sheltie for a while, but he was acting increasingly aggressive toward our three-year-old, so we had to return the dog to his owner.

It was early June that year when our six-year-old decided she was ready for a pet. Not wanting anymore dog problems, we told her it wasn't time. That was when she got creative and decided a beetle would make a good pet! That is correct—a beetle! She had studied them in school and wanted to bring one home.

"Mom, they are quiet. It won't disturb the neighbors!" she said. "Dad, it won't shed all over the way Abby did! We can play barefoot in the backyard!"

Clearly, a beetle was the way to go!

We discovered that beetles are extremely low maintenance! A few drops of water and fresh leaves keep a beetle going for several days! In case you are thinking about taking in a beetle as a pet, I warn you that they are not fond of spiders that may accidentally enter the jar on those fresh leaves!

Sadly, in mid-July, we discovered the beetle had gone to that great garden in the sky. How did we know? A fuzzy beetle is not a healthy beetle! When Jillian heard it was dead, she simply said, "Now it can be in my dead bug collection!"

After Abby's passing, our three year-old occasionally asked me and Russ questions about death. Like many preschoolers, he was fascinated with dinosaurs, how they had "left their bones behind." After the dog died, he asked, "What happened to her bones?"

We explained that because we lived in a parsonage, we had no place to bury Abby so she was cremated. That is what the Bible talks about: "For dust you are and to dust you will return" (Genesis 3:19, NIV). "But where are her bones?" he asked.

"Oh, they're up on that shelf," I said, pointing!

Whether it's a beetle or a dog, your child, your spouse, or you, death comes. I am not saying we handled it correctly, and those were pets, not people. I *am* saying you *do* have to handle it, prepare for it, and expect it. This is why all of life is held with an open hand. "For dust you are and to dust you will return."

Our attitude determines how we handle life. We *can* arrive at the point where we accept all things peacefully if we know this life is not all there is. This reassuring promise is found in Romans 5:17 (NIV): "The sin of this one man, Adam, caused death to rule over many. But even greater is God's wonderful grace and his gift of righteousness, for all who receive it will live in triumph over sin and death through this one man, Jesus Christ."

Don't you want to triumph over sin and death? The strength and courage to do so are found in Jesus who has gone before us and won the battle. Our fears and worries about death can and should be put to rest.

The expression, "It's better than the alternative," is used when one is speaking of something unpleasant. The person is saying he would rather suffer through one thing than die. But why suffer and live when nothing is better than heaven? Certainly, the process of getting to heaven can be excruciating, and I hope that is all people mean when they use the expression. Sometimes I think they are saying this life is better than heaven, and it simply is not true! The glory God has prepared for us is unsurpassed and makes this life as less than nothing.

My sister came in contact with many lovely people during her illness. Their faith and prayers encouraged her. At the same time, many people struggled. Their conflicted feelings are very understandable; illness can strike anyone at any time. Barb's illness forced them to come to terms with their mortality … or not.

Barb managed most of her own care while she was able. She arranged doctors' appointments and called friends who said, "Call anytime you need anything." While they were all probably well-intentioned offers, very few people followed through when assistance was needed.

Barb called a friend and asked her to come to the house and read the Bible to her. The friend said she could not come. I asked Barb if she was angry with all the dead ends, and she said, "Not angry...." What emotion was she feeling? I can only imagine it was sympathy, disappointment, or loneliness.

Their busy schedules were to blame for their inability to assist. Barb simply called another number. She never faulted anyone; she did not complain. She was always gracious and never lost her ability to overlook friends' unreliability.

People face their own mortality when around a dying person. Many cannot deal with the knowledge that this could happen to them. Even longtime church members are uneasy about death. I once heard Billy Graham say that he looks forward to heaven but not the process of dying. It is a painful course for most; people are understandably reticent. One of Barb's friends said she would no longer visit because seeing Barb in that condition was too difficult for her. Barb cried for days afterward.

A dying person's ability to cope with the gradual loss of health, mobility, and bodily functions is all the change one should have to bear. A slipping away of the support system should not be part of the process.

The reality is that not everyone possesses the skills and experience to walk with someone "through the valley of the shadow." While there are exceptions to every rule, these suggestions may help friends, neighbors, and even relatives feel more comfortable when they are interacting with dying people:

1. When you desire to visit, inquire whether the patient feels up to having company. If he or she does, keep the visit brief. Watch for cues. If the patient no longer participates in conversation, he or she may be tired. The most loving thing to do is leave so that he or she can rest.

2. Do not bring children who may become loud and unruly unless the family gives permission in advance. The sight of an extremely ill person can frighten children and create anxiety in the patient. The patient needs a calm environment.

3. Meals are deeply appreciated by a family consumed with caregiving. Do not assume the only food an ill person can eat is soup! Variety is nice. Ask what the family and patient are

hungry for and drop it off by 5:00 p.m. in case they desire an early meal.

4. Telephone calls can disrupt long-sought rest, but greeting cards with cheerful notes, Facebook inquiries, and e-mails can be addressed at opportune times.

5. Keep emotions in check. Crying can easily discourage one who is already feeling down. Visit with the goal of encouraging and cheering the patient. Put her or his needs first.

6. One of my favorite Bible passages says comfort as you've been comforted (2 Corinthians 1:4). This sounds like my children's paraphrase of the second greatest commandment: Treat others the way you want to be treated (Matthew 22:39). Remember, in other words, how suffering has felt in your life and respond with the same compassion you received.

The good-bye process is not easy. My father left us suddenly because of a massive heart attack. Barb's lingering, agonizing death was gut-wrenching. An unexpected passing shocks the family and is most difficult for them, but this may be the best for the dying person because the suffering is brief. There is time to come to terms with the inevitability of the ensuing death when a loved one suffers over months or years. Either way, there is suffering.

Grieving families are fertile ground for ministry. People are often receptive to the seeds of truth and faith that can be planted. Pray for yourself and find strength to be the friend to the ill person in the same way you have been to the healthy ones in your life.

Chapter Eight

Portions of Barb's Facebook
Page for Your Inspiration

This sheet was given out at Barb's funeral. She posted these thoughts on her Facebook page throughout her illness.

After you have suffered a little while, our God, who is full of kindness through Christ, will give you His eternal glory. He personally will come and pick you up, set you firmly in place, and make you stronger than ever. (1 Peter 5:10, TLB). August 22 at 5:33 p.m.

For I am the Lord, your God, who takes hold of your right hand and says to you. Do not fear; I will help you. (Isaiah 41:13, NIV) August 23 at 10:12 a.m.

My favorite comment in the past few weeks: Caroline sat on her daddy's lap and said, "Daddy, no matter how many womanly chores you do, I will always call you Daddy." August 31 at 4:16 p.m.

If children have the ability to ignore all odds and percentages, then maybe we can all learn from them. When you think about it, what other choice is there but to hope? We have two options, medically and emotionally: Give up or fight like hell. —Lance Armstrong. September 1 at 12:31 a.m.

My husband is so amazing that even though he hates to play Scrabble, he bought me a new board—one that has snap in letters that we can play together—and the letters will still be intact when I start nodding off. September 4 at 10:12 p.m.

Surely, God is my salvation; I will trust and not be afraid. The LORD, the LORD is my strength and my song; He has become my salvation. (Isaiah 12:2, NIV). September 8 at 8:46 p.m.

I am not contagious. September 8 at 10:04 p.m.

Friend's response: Not unless you count your amazing outlook on life and your love of Christ. Then I'd have to say you are amazingly inspirational and contagious as all get out! September 8 at 10:08 p.m.

Barb's reply: Well thanks, but you give me too much credit. I don't post the times when I am scared to death and have to get myself refocused and remind myself who the great physician really is. September 8 at 10:33 p.m.

Sorry I am doing just little updates at a time, but that is all I am up to right now. Rested so comfortably at the hospital this a.m. before the procedure that Caroline was determined that I needed a hospital bed at home. It was ordered, delivered, and set up before 5:00 p.m. That was when it hit me. I really am sick, and this is going to be long term. September 10 at 7:50 p.m.

I lift up my eyes to the hills—where does my help come from? My help comes from the LORD, the maker of heaven and earth. (Psalm 121:1–2, NIV). September 11 at 6:46 p.m.

So this is what it feels like—this mass has grabbed hold of every muscle and nerve in my hip and thigh and is just squeezing and pulling. It is not being very nice. September 13 at 8:13 a.m.

Tomorrow is the big day. We find out what this monster is inside me and what we are going to do to fight it. Remember, the doctor does not want to do surgery in that region. So we are praying that chemo/radiation is the treatment plan. It's in God's hands, and we are as ready as we can be to face it. Pray for strength for my family please and for relief of this stress we have been under. Love my family and friends so much. September 15 at 8:30 p.m.

Off to see what the next few months (and more) hold for me. September 16 at 8:15 a.m.

A great time of praise and worship with part of my Etna UMC family (just what I needed). September 19 at 6:25 p.m.

This is what I have been learning: If we slow down long enough to give *and* we slow down long enough to receive, life is amazing. There are people wanting to give and people needing to receive. When you get that right match together … the outcome is unbelievable. Thank you, dear friends and family. September 19 at 9:57 p.m.

Feels like I have prayer warriors "sea to shining sea." I know I have prayers being said for me in OH, NC, WV, IL, FL, GA, and CA. Where else am I being covered? September 21 at 10:38 a.m. South Carolina, Minnesota, Washington, Oregon, Utah, Michigan, Tennessee, Kentucky, Colorado, New Hampshire, England, and Virginia.

We are so pleased with all of the surgical team at OSU. I have never been around so many people who are so genuinely concerned about my care. September 23 at 10:09 a.m.

Here goes my reputation for being positive … I don't even know how to pray today. September 26 at 9:29 p.m.

I just saw that one of our dear friends is using a picture of our family as her profile pic as a reminder to pray for us throughout the day. Isn't that an amazing thing to do? It's the little things people are doing that are just wowing me. October 14 at 12:26 a.m.

Mothers of teenage daughters, be jealous! I have the perfect teenage daughter right here who has stepped up to a whole new level on what it means to love and honor your parents. October 14 at 3:18 p.m.

I have an amazing family. October 23 at 5:55 p.m.

Wish one of my family members would read their Facebook and bring me a banana. October 25 at 10:40 p.m.

Message from a Facebook site called *God Wants You to Know:* On **this day, God** wants you to know that how bad things may look right now means nothing; it's how good they can be with God's help that counts. In life, you can absolutely count on one thing—everything can turn around in one day, in one minute sometimes. Don't you dare to give up; you might be a moment away from a windfall. November 20 at 11:23 a.m.

Message from a Facebook site called *God Wants You to Know:* **On this day, God** wants you to know that today you have a cause for celebration. Today, you should celebrate what an unbelievable life you have had so far: the accomplishments, the many blessings, and yes, even the hardships because they have served to make you stronger. Just as a gem cannot be polished without friction, nor can a life be perfected without trials. Take time to acknowledge your life and to praise yourself. December 2 at 2:23 p.m.

Love you so so so so so so so so so so so so so so so so so so so so so so so so so so so so so so so so so so so so so so so so so so so so so much! You will *always* be with me, and I will *always* be with you! You are my hero. December 2 at 5:40 p.m.

I have the *best* mama in the whole world! She is so very strong and dedicated in her faith and love. I hope God doesn't take her from us too soon. But no matter what, Barb Ohlinger (Mama), you will *always* be my hero. December 9 at 8:46 p.m.

No love, no friendship can ever cross our path without affecting us in some way forever. —Author unknown

Chapter 9

⟞⟋

Barb's Eulogy: Touched by Living Water

Acommunity mourns this day. One doesn't have to be an elected official or hold a prominent position to make a difference. Just impact the world one soul at a time. Barb did.

Her intelligence and love for children merged at Ohio State University, where she wanted to become a teacher but did the next best thing: She taught, loved, and nurtured little ones who have grown and are growing into responsible adults. What a gift to this community! Will you hold those eighty-seven children in your prayers? They may not understand it yet, but they were blessed to be guided by one from whose life flowed living water—that is, the spirit of Jesus, who flows from one and refreshes hundreds (Oswald Chambers, "My Utmost for His Highest," devotional from September 2). We pause to thank God for this woman who *touched* us with *living water*.

Let us pray.

Today, Loving Father, we say good-bye to one who left too soon. Yet, we confidently release her to your tender, loving care because her faith in Jesus was genuine and engaging. Refreshing, life-giving water—the spirit of your Son—flowed from Barb's heart. Cause her life to be our lesson in faithful, righteous living. We pray in the name of Jesus, our Savior. Amen.

Barb lived her life devoted to her family and to her Lord, a wonderful combination of Mary and Martha, the sisters in the gospels who were Jesus's friends.

She was Martha the homemaker who was a coupon cutter and also loved blue and M&M's. So when she found a coupon on Facebook for free blue M&M's, she ordered them embossed with "Fish Fry" for the annual Labor Day weekend family gathering. Barb did enjoy chocolate! When teaching Caroline to bake, they unwrapped the Hershey's kisses as Barb demonstrated, "Eat one, bake with one, eat one, bake with one." They had to make a Kroger run for more kisses!

She was a creative cook who doctored recipes until she liked them. Whenever she experimented, she asked Michael, "Is it a keeper or a throwaway?" She also put her creativity to use in making crafts. Years ago, we all received Christmas stockings with our names on them. Once she sewed Caroline a pair of pants inside out and backward. They laughed about it for a week, and then Barb fixed them! Each year, she makes her special hot chocolate mix for Christmas gifts.

She was Martha the homemaker. But she was also Mary, the follower of Jesus, who sat at his feet to soak in His wisdom and love (Luke 10:39–40).

When Caroline was born and she was so tiny, Barb and Michael contacted this church (Etna United Methodist in Etna, Ohio). Pastor Tim Burden visited and they felt a connection with him and began attending. Their relationship with this congregation grew, and Barb created summer music camp for dozens of children annually among many other ministries.

Her Bible knowledge grew, and she didn't hesitate to point out scripture to me when she believed I needed reminding!

The opportunity to experience the deep and abiding faith of Barb, Michael, Caroline, and Ginny over the past year was extremely inspiring. They are a close family, and their Lord and Savior Jesus Christ is a very real part of that closeness.

Michael is the eternal optimist, and his faith makes him that way. He looks for the best in everything and everybody, and his witness to the Lord is strong. How fortunate Barb was to have you these twenty-five years. You gave her everything she wanted, even when it meant painting the living room a color called *necturina*, carrying home five gallons of orange paint because she loved the color!

Ginny is a mother-in-law who cares like a mother. Thank you. She was always ready to assist when needs arose. Ginny was a gift to Barb these past months.

Caroline, you had a treasure not many people receive: Your mother was home with you all of your life, and you have logged countless hours together. She did it because she understood the importance of family. You seem to read each other's thoughts, so close is your bond. You have grown into a mature young woman these last months. This was profoundly obvious the day of the first biopsy. You saw how comfortably your mama rested in that hospital bed, and before we knew it, you were in the nurse's station on their computer, searching for a hospital bed supplier! One was delivered that evening!

Last December when your mama wanted to plan this service, she paused in the middle of the planning, grew teary-eyed, and said, "I can't believe I'm doing this!"

Without hesitation, you asked, "Want to do mine, too?" That's how you've been—always there for her, always helpful, always a source of pride. What a precious daughter you are.

Barb was a wonderful example for us all. Her humor saw us all through these months.

Even when she was a teenager, she was able to make light of a situation. She was sick; it may have been when she fell off a step and broke her foot. She stood on the back porch and sang to our parents: "What do you get when you get real sick? You get a bunch of hospital bills. That's what you get for all your pills. I'll never get sick again. I'll never get sick again" (Barb's version of "I'll Never Fall in Love Again" by The Carpenters).

Barb fought the good fight without complaint. In fact, over these months, her humor kept us going. December 29, she went for her first transfusion. Transferring from the car to the wheelchair was difficult. In the midst of struggling to pivot on her strong leg, she exclaimed, "I'm a dainty ballerina!"

October 7, the night Dr. Mayerson revealed the diagnosis, I called Barb at James around 9:30. Michael put her on, and she chanted, "*I get to see Dad before you do!*"

No amount of pain could quench her spirit or cause the living water to stop flowing. It was the spirit of Jesus, who flowed from her in the form of laughter and kindness, friendship and warmth, and the opening of her home to all because she knew *we* needed it. The love of Jesus touched us through her.

Barb taught us that cancer doesn't quench the spirit,
    cancer doesn't lessen our humor,
    cancer doesn't swallow our joy,
    cancer doesn't decrease our love,
    cancer doesn't diminish our positive attitude,

cancer doesn't hinder our friendships,
cancer doesn't darken our emotions,
cancer doesn't steal our faith,
cancer doesn't rob us of hope,
cancer doesn't harm our relationship with Jesus.
(Based on the poem "What Cancer Cannot Do," author
unknown.)

But cancer *has* taught us a profound lesson about how temporary life is because we didn't know twelve months ago we'd be here today.

God supplies our needs instantaneously, any moment, anywhere. Tuesday at 5:45 a.m., Jesus said, "Barb, welcome to my world." So, we let her go. We give her to God. We wouldn't want to take her from the joy she is experiencing now for anything.

The Bible paints vague pictures of the world beyond life, and we won't completely understand the joy of eternal life until we receive it ourselves. That is why we want to be the most faithful people we can be—loving, forgiving, kind, putting the Lord first and others second and ourselves last, loving others as we love ourselves.

Altar Call

Last August, Barb gave very specific instructions for this point in her service. It was extremely important to her. In fact, she asked to read this on June 12 to be sure it communicated her intended message.

We've all been touched by the living water that flowed out of Barb. She wants you to understand today in a way that perhaps you've never understood that Jesus is the source of everything loving and gracious in her. God's Son died for her sins and ours, and everyone who trusts in Jesus lives forever with Him. That is the victory she has won. *She is present with Jesus.*

Can she see us? Certainly, she is here today. I believe that heaven is someplace very near. There will be times when you will sense Barb's presence because she is nearby. The relationship isn't over; it has changed. She is seated in the grandstands of heaven, cheering us on (Hebrews 12:1). She is Caroline's greatest cheerleader!

That living water continues to flow from Barb to you in the form of a personal request. She wants to see you all in heaven. She wants you to be there. She wants you all to leave here confident and assured of your place in paradise.

She wants you to have that "river of life" flowing out of you.

She wants you to know Jesus as Savior and Lord, not as a halfhearted commitment but as a life-altering reality.

She wants you to make a commitment to Jesus today. Barb understood it's not enough to be a good person or to lead a good life. She knew the living-water faith requires a transformation of the heart and mind. She knew that no one earns a ticket to heaven. No one inherits the family faith. A conscious, deliberate commitment is required.

So will you ask yourself a couple of questions: Have I placed my faith in Christ as Savior? Have I invited Him to live in me and flow through me?

Knowing that you'll all join her in heaven someday made this transition much calmer for her.

Barb wants you all to commit or recommit your lives to Jesus. She wants you to come to the altar and humble yourself before the Lord. Repent of the old way and take on the way of Jesus. Your life will be new, better, different! You'll grow to understand that this life is not about you. You are on the planet to glorify God in every situation. The spirit of Jesus will enter your heart, and living water will run through you and out of you. And consequently, hundreds will be touched. You will be transformed.

Won't you come to the altar and pray? The Lord will meet you wherever you are spiritually.

Barb knew we couldn't all fit at the altar at once; you'll have to take turns! Kneel in the aisle. Stand if you can't kneel. When one sits down, another can come forward.

This is your moment, one set aside in all eternity to come to Jesus. Barb has chosen a special song for this moment. Let this be your "Defining Moment."

Prayer

Our loving, gracious God, today we celebrate the life of one who left us too soon, one whose love for you was real, deep, abiding. We are grateful that she has moved to a new way of living where Jesus Himself wiped every tear from her eyes, a place where there is no more death or mourning or crying or pain (Revelation 21:4). Thank you, Lord. Her pain has ended! Our Christian faith teaches that something more glorious than we can imagine is awaiting us. When approaching the end, we face the beginning. So we praise you for the new and everlasting life Barb has received. How so very like her to be concerned about *us* in the midst of her horrendous battle.

As hearts are open to you now, forgive our sins and receive us as your children. Give those who desire new life the salvation they seek. Recreate them in the image of your Son. Keep us all on the path that leads to life eternal. We pray through your Son, our Savior, Jesus Christ. Amen.

Chapter 9

⸻

Dove Ceremony

Pastors have the unique privilege of participating in life's high moments: baptisms, confirmation, weddings, and funerals. At the end of every cemetery committal service, I say to the family, "Thank you for the privilege of sharing in this day." I really mean that. Families invite pastors into their world for life's most sacred events, and the invitation is not taken lightly.

The most meaningful committal service I have witnessed occurred at Barb's burial. Richard S. Hoskinson of Hoskinson Funeral Home in Kirkersville, Ohio, has a wonderful dove ceremony he sometimes uses at committal services. We were so pleased he chose to include the ritual when Barb was laid to rest.

At the conclusion of the pastor's portion of the service, the funeral director invited friends and family to step outside the tent. There, perhaps fifty feet away, stood a woman with a basket. He began reading scripture: "We would rather be away from these earthly bodies, for then we will be at home with the Lord" (2 Corinthians 5:8, NLT).

The woman released three homing doves that represent the Holy Trinity: the Father, Son, and Holy Spirit. They immediately flew toward the funeral home, where they roost. One was a mate of the fourth dove, and because they mate for life, the dove circled back to retrieve his mate. When the fourth dove was released, the bird represented Barb flying home to her creator, God. Mr. Hoskinson then proclaimed, "My Father's house has many rooms … I am going there to prepare a place for you. And if I go and prepare a place for you, I will come back and take you to be with me that you also may be where I am" (John 14:2–3, NIV).

What a beautiful, moving, inspiring sight! We saw the four doves flying into the distance as Mr. Hoskinson read, "Oh, that I had the wings of a dove" (Psalm 55:6, NIV).

Such powerful and moving imagery! Praise be to God for the gift of eternal life, which is offered through His Son, Jesus Christ!

Afterword

Nothing prepares the family left behind for those unanticipated moments when ongoing life slaps them with reminders of their loved one's absence:

- How empty the house is without her!
- The shopping list changes; no one else drinks chocolate milk and Mug Root Beer.
- Two-year-old granddaughter Jenna remembers Barb as "Sleeping Grandma" because she was often in bed.
- Her texts remain on my cell phone as a private collection, a piece of Barb that no one else has. Her Facebook page still receives comments from friends missing her. Caroline has saved her final voice-mail message.
- The last ChapStick and makeup Barb used are in Caroline's "Mama Drawer."
- The nearly empty bottle of honey mustard salad dressing is in the fridge; no one else uses it, and no one can throw it out.
- New checks were ordered, but it was too soon to remove her name.
- Caroline wears her socks because "I find joy in wearing them."
- Caroline told her mother in a coherent moment shortly before her death that she is changing her college major to nursing. Barb's illness was the inspiration. Barb smiled and said, "That's so good. I'm so happy for you. You'll be great at it." Michael indicates that Barb always believed Caroline would go into nursing.

- Seven months after her mama's death, Caroline sang a solo in worship once again. Her mama wasn't there to offer the customary post-performance hug, and she was deeply missed; however, Barb surely cheered her on from the grandstands of heaven.

Time is now divided into before and after July 19, 2011. Barb's new beginning vanquishes the grief. Prayer continues to sustain the family. Laughter remains in their home just as she would want.